LOVE PRESCRIPTION FOR RELATIONSHIP

How to woo someone into loving you.

Michael Walker

Contents

Chapter 1 : BEING LOVABLE

Chapter 2: GETTING READY FOR EMOTIONAL DIFFICULTY

Chapter 3: DEVELOPING A BOND

Chapter 4: RESPECT AND LOVING YOUR PARTNER

Chapter 5: MAINTAINING THEIR LOVE

Chapter 6: BEGINNING A ROMANCE

Bottom line

Chapter 1 : BEING LOVABLE

Everything is about love! It is the source of all of our energy, sustaining both us and the environment in which we live.
How can we entice more love to us? by becoming more endearing?
We may attract the kind of love we want by being lovable. Being more likable enables us to draw meaningful, real love, whether it is romantic love or a deeper love with friends and family.

So how do we improve our love ability?

Initially, you fall in love with yourself.
For some of us, falling in love with ourselves can be difficult. It's worth it, though. It's critical to spend time doing the things that make you happy, to ignore the critical voice in your head, and to quit dwelling on the past if you want to leap.

You will then begin to draw the limitless love that every one of us deserves.

Self-care is important. The way someone looks has a major impact on whether or not they will find someone attractive. People can immediately tell how well you take care of your physical health and looks, therefore it is worthwhile to invest some extra time and effort in this area when you are attempting to attract someone. If you don't take care of yourself, people will notice, and they can lose interest.

Exercise, eat healthily, maintain good cleanliness, and dress in neat, flattering attire to look your best.

Never be scared to draw attention to yourself.

Make a name for yourself, accomplish something noteworthy, and demonstrate to them that you are much more than simply a gorgeous face with a smile.

Make sure your personality comes through and that he or she is aware of your preferences. People find it incredibly attractive when you are passionate about something.
Take pride in your accomplishments and have self-assurance in your skills. People admire confidence, so don't be embarrassed to brag about your accomplishments.

Be considerate. Treat people how you would like to be treated. Although it may be corny, it is true. You need to start treating other people with care and respect if you expect others to do the same for you. People that have wonderful personalities, are polite, and are kind to others are more likely to make someone fall in love with them.

Display your shortcomings. Let him or her witness your progress. Tell the person about your transformation, for instance, if you used to be a couch potato but are now fit and active. Someone will respect you more if

you let them in on some of your past failings
so be open with them

Chapter 2: GETTING READY FOR EMOTIONAL DIFFICULTY

We all require emotional support.
Think about the necessities of life, such as food, shelter, air, and water. You can maintain your physical survival by taking care of basic necessities, but meaningful living requires more.
Companionship, tenderness, security, and appreciation are things that cannot be seen or touched but are yet just as valuable. The same is true for feeling respected or heard.

If you and your partner in a relationship have a strong link, that will likely affect how well your needs are addressed.

Acting unconcerned about the relationship is not acceptable. They do this so frequently. It docsn't help and makes the other person feel like a burden, so pretending that you don't care or aren't bothered about the relationship won't work.

Be sensitive and available. Relations are challenging. Make sure you are prepared for a relationship before attempting to woo someone. Don't try to make someone fall in love with you if you are too attached to a former relationship, more interested in dating someone else, or simply not ready for commitment.

Consider whether you are really in love. This might be it. Think about your feelings for this person. Do you cherish them? You should be sure that you have romantic feelings for the person and not just a strong friendship. Often, it might be challenging to distinguish between the two. Consider taking things slowly if you haven't fallen in love with the person yet. If it's meant to be, you'll feel things for one other.

Consider your motivations. Consider your reasons for wanting to be in a relationship. Getting someone to fall in love with you is a horrible idea if all you want from them is to feel better about ending another connection with them or to make someone else jealous. This is irresponsible given the very real emotions kids might experience. Go forward if you want someone to fall in love with you because you want to be with them for a very long time and have a relationship that is supportive of both parties.

Think about your aims. Set long-term objectives for the relationship. Making someone fall in love with you doesn't make much sense if you don't see it lasting. This is cruel to both you and the other person emotionally. There is nothing wrong with casual dating; just enjoy it for what it is and don't attempt to make it more serious if you want to date someone but don't see it lasting. To continue dating, you don't have to be in love.

Recognize that there are others. Sometimes the feelings we have for someone are not reciprocated. This is alright. There shouldn't be any sense of hopelessness or loneliness on your part. After all, there are a lot of people in our world. You should accept that it wasn't meant to be and that you wouldn't have been very happy together if someone doesn't reciprocate your sentiments. Before you know it, you'll find someone else and wonder why you ever felt sad in the first place.
Try not to pretend to be someone you are not to win someone over. Make sure the person you choose to be with can accept you for who you are.

These 10 emotional requirements are an excellent place to start when determining whether you and your spouse are individually receiving what you need from the relationship, even though every relationship is a little bit different.

1.Affection

In most partnerships, there are various forms of affection:

physical contact

sexual affinities

Kind deeds and warm words

You can bond and become more intimate by showing affection.

Although not everyone expresses affection in the same ways, couples typically grow accustomed to each other's individual methods of meeting this desire.

Someone who doesn't express their love verbally may do so in other ways, such as through their behavior.

You can begin to worry if your relationship's amount of affection abruptly shifts. It's very understandable to ask why a once-affectionate partner now looks distant or avoidant of contact, as many relationship problems are the result of a loss of affection.

A dialogue is a wonderful place to start if they appear less loving than normal. Keep in mind that you can't know what's going on without asking.

Try taking a non-aggressive stance:

"Recently, I've noticed some distance. I feel alone when we can't communicate through touch. If you don't feel up to physical affection right now, I wonder if there's a way we could communicate instead through words.

2.Acceptance

Being in a relationship with someone who accepts you for who you are might help you feel a sense of belonging.

But being accepted doesn't only mean that someone likes you. Additionally, it implies that you feel as though you belong in their life and blend in with their family.

This sense of belonging could become stronger if they:

invite your relatives and friends to visit you organize joint activities, discuss future aspirations and aspirations, and seek counsel when making decisions.

You can feel like you're on the periphery of their life if you don't feel like you're accepted. It's uncomfortable to be here.

Some people find it difficult to open up, and they can have other excuses for keeping you out of some aspects of their lives.

Nevertheless, it could be challenging for you to envision yourself remaining in the relationship over the long run if you feel unwelcome.

Try the following tactic: If you haven't done so before, arrange for them to meet your friends and family. Start a discussion about how you'd like to be more active in their life using this as a starting point.

3. Assurance

Even the closest partners do not always agree, and that is acceptable. Even if you don't quite concur, you still want to be sure that your worries have been heard and that they are aware of your perspective.

Most couples believe it's critical to communicate on the same wavelength, according to data by 2016 Trusted Source. You could feel misunderstood if your companion utterly fails to understand your viewpoint. You might feel neglected or mistreated if they completely ignore your feelings.

If this only occurs occasionally but you normally feel validated, it's conceivable that they were having a bad day. Regardless, it doesn't harm to talk to someone about how you're feeling.

However, if you frequently feel dismissed or invalidated, you can start to harbor animosity, so it's best to confront the situation as soon as possible.

Try:

When I raise significant problems lately, I don't feel like I'm being heard. Could we arrange a time when we could both listen attentively to serious discussions?

4. Self-rule

Partners frequently start sharing interests, hobbies, and other facets of daily life as a relationship develops. As you get closer, you might realize that you're coming together more.

But regardless of how solid your connection develops, it's crucial to preserve your sense of self. Although you may share a lot of similarities, you are still two distinct individuals with separate values and a different sets of interests, friends, and aspirations.

Take a step back and assess the situation if you notice that your identity is beginning to meld with theirs. This merging of identities can take place organically as you get closer, but it can also occur if you think you need to change for the relationship to work.

In fact, sticking to your unique interests might encourage curiosity about one another, which can improve your relationship and keep things interesting. Set aside some time to catch up with friends or pick up an old activity if you find yourself losing sight of who you were before the relationship.

5. Safety
Although security can mean many different things, it should always feel safe in a partnership.

If your relationship is safe, you typically:

understand that they respect your boundaries
Feel free to express your emotions.
Feel physically safe with them and think they respect your decisions.
feel comfortable sharing your emotions
Setting clear limits might increase your sense of security:

If you raise your voice, I won't answer because I don't want to be shouted at.
If your partner starts to abuse you, get professional help. Physical violence is

frequently obvious to spot, but mental abuse can also make you feel frightened, even if you're not sure why.

6. Trust

Security and trust frequently go hand in hand. Being emotionally or physically secure with someone you can't trust is difficult. When you trust someone, you may be confident that they have your best interests in mind.

Try bringing up particular actions, such as staying out late without an explanation, if you start to have doubts about them. This assists in addressing communication demands while assisting in getting to the bottom of what is happening.

Trust generally takes time to develop. It takes time to grow, but it may also be lost in an instant. Broken trust can occasionally be restored, but doing so involves work on the parts of both spouses and frequently, assistance from a therapist.

Be clear about your policies for handling betrayals of trust in the partnership. You probably have a decent sense of the behaviors you can't accept, like cheating or lying, even though your specific response may change according to the circumstances. Don't feel bad about telling your partner about those red flags.

7. Compassion

Empathy is the ability to put yourself in someone else's shoes. This skill is necessary for romantic relationships since it fosters mutual understanding and stronger bonding.

Claim that they missed your birthday. You experience hurt and rage. How could they after being together for 5 years? Never have you overlooked their birthday.

But once the disappointment and rage have subsided, you begin to see their point of view. They've been having trouble at work lately, and their nervousness has started to keep them up at night. The majority of their emotional energy has been invested in organizing a significant task that might help things get better.

You argue that it's easier to understand how they forgot all about your birthday with all of the stuff on their minds. You are aware that they are hurt and that it wasn't done on purpose.

Understanding their predicament enables you to accept what happened and extend mercy and forgiveness to them, which can deepen your relationship. On the other hand, continuing to stew can cause you to disagree or cause other problems.

8. Setting priorities

To desire your partner to put you first is rather common. You want to know that when they tend to their own needs, yours will come next.

Of course, the majority of people have one or more meaningful relationships. Every now and again, someone else in their life might need to take precedences, such as a buddy going through a crisis or a relative going through a difficult time.

But generally, you'll assume that they don't actually value your presence if you don't feel like a priority in their life. You could start to wonder why they even maintain the relationship in light of this.

A discussion is frequently beneficial. Start by explaining why you don't feel prioritized; use an I-statement to stop yourself from coming off as judgmental. They might ignore your texts for a day or two or keep canceling date nights to catch up with buddies.

Then offer a potential solution, such as returning phone calls or text messages each evening, scheduling a regular date night, etc.

9. Relationship

It's acceptable to not do everything together. In actuality, pursuing distinct hobbies and friendships can benefit both your relationship and your mental health (see autonomy above).

However, you also want to feel a sense of connection. That makes complete sense. What other purpose does sharing your life serve in relationships?

Even if you spend the majority of your time together, loneliness can still exist without connection. You may be just two people who happen to live together or occasionally spend time together. There's a strong chance you don't want your relationship to develop that way.

The good thing is that you can engage with them again if you don't feel like you're connected to them.

Some good advice:

Ask them about a facet of their daily life you've never given much thought to.
Offer the group a novel activity to try.
Take a day or weekend getaway to change things up from your typical routine.
Share childhood recollections or trade personal ones to strengthen your relationship.
10. Space Space is vital, but so is connection.

When there is room for a partnership, both people are free to pursue their own interests whenever they wish. Although you realize you can make your own decisions, you feel supported.

Additionally, it implies that you still get some privacy. This privacy can refer to distinct living quarters for working or unwinding, but it can also refer to emotional privacy.

Being truthful does not require you to express every idea that enters your head. Getting some emotional and physical distance might help you deal with negative emotions, such as annoyance, without taking it out on your partner.

It's important to ask for what you need when it comes to space.

Consider:

establishing a quiet space for oneself at homes, such as a separate room or a little nook, and scheduling some time alone each day outside

Chapter 3: DEVELOPING A BOND

When a relationship first begins, we're usually quite good about carving out time for one another, but as life gets in the way and we become too comfortable, our connection falters and we end up spending less time together. It need not be expensive or time-consuming to find ways to rekindle your relationship with your partner, but doing so supports a happy, solid, and healthy partnership. Here are some suggestions for strengthening your relationship with your significant other.

Learn more about the person. Getting to know someone better and letting them get to know you is the first step in winning their heart. It takes time and effort to get to know someone because you need to ask the appropriate questions and listen attentively.

Find out what your potential partner aspired to be when they were younger and what they want to accomplish now. You can learn about the person's aims, dreams, and other aspirations for their life through this.
Inquire about preferences, inclinations, pursuits, and hobbies.

Embrace the person's interests. Take an interest in the things that the person you are dating like, and educate yourself on what makes them happy. Don't pretend to be interested in something since others can usually tell when you aren't. Try to share in the person's passion and experience their interests through their eyes. This will offer you a common interest and set you on the road to romance.
Ask them to explain more about it or show you how to play, for instance, if they are a great fan of a sport you don't know much (or anything) about. Alternately, if the other person is very into a certain genre of music,

listen to a lot of it and look for songs you both enjoy.

Think of the guy as a hero. When they are near you, make your partner feel like your hero. Allow them to assist you with your academic work so they can feel accomplished, seek their personal counsel so they can feel knowledgeable, and request assistance or advice on any issues that are particularly significant to them (to give them a chance to demonstrate expertise). Making your significant other feel helpful and capable can also be accomplished by asking for assistance with clothing choices or reaching or opening containers.

Establish trust. A solid, sustainable relationship must have trust as a foundation. Learn to trust your partner and demonstrate that trust through your words and deeds. Make sure you demonstrate to your partner that you are trustworthy as well.

Keep a secret that your partner has told you. Don't bring up or make fun of them if you learn something embarrassing about them.
With your partner, expose pieces of yourself that only they see. Share your secrets with them. With your significant partner, you should feel free to be vulnerable and let them console you.

When your partner is going through a tough period, support them. Assisting is crucial in developing genuine love between two people. The majority of people seek out partnerships because they enjoy having someone to lean on. If you can show your significant other that you care about and support them, it will go a long way toward making them fall in love with you.
You might offer to merely listen and offer physical comfort at times to support someone. Sometimes, though, you might need to take additional action. For instance, you might need to assist your significant

other with their studies if they are having trouble in class.

Respect is the understanding that the other person is a whole individual and not merely a means to an end. It implies that you are aware of and accept your partner's diverse experiences and viewpoints from your own.

While expressing respect for someone is simple, really acting in that manner might be more challenging. I want to discuss how you can respect others in your relationship in this book because of this. After all, simply because you don't threaten or verbally abuse your partner does not imply that you are treating them with respect.

Here are six ways you may respect and adore your partner. What more would you say?

1. Exhibit trust.
Even non-romantic relationships require trust to function. However, trust is much

more than just believing that your lover won't be unfaithful to you. Acting out your trust in your partner is far more effective than just feeling it.

You can show your lover that you trust them by not continually contacting or texting them. Instead, give them one SMS or call. Tell them you're thinking about them and hope to hear from them soon in your message. This demonstrates your faith in them to get in touch with you when they can and your knowledge that your spouse values your efforts.

It should go without saying, but never search through your partner's personal belongings or phone without their consent. Talk to them if you get the strange impression that they're trying to keep something from you. If there is no drama, there is no need to create it!

2. Pay attention to your communication style.

One of the hardest and most crucial aspects of a relationship is communication. Because being open and honest with your spouse also involves being honest with yourself, this is the case.

Expecting your mate to read your mind is unrealistic. When you're upset, it's crucial to discuss your concerns openly. Don't accuse anyone. Make remarks that start with "I," such as, "I feel terribly disregarded and irrelevant when you cancel our plans at the last minute," or "I feel irritated when you continuously ask me to hang out when you know I need to study." When people respect my time, it means a lot to me. Remember that your feelings are always valid and don't feel terrible about them.

Everyone occasionally disagrees, and that is entirely acceptable. Don't disappear or stop communicating when you do. Tell your partner at the very least that you're upset and need some time to collect your thoughts before speaking. They won't feel as though you abandoned them or didn't care about their sentiments as a result. By stating words like "I understand why you feel that way" or "I hear what you're saying," you can validate your partner's emotions.

But communication extends beyond words. You can show your significant other that you care by donning their favorite scent, listening to their favorite music together, or bringing them flowers.

3. Be trustworthy and responsible.
Trust is a crucial component of every relationship, but it's difficult to have faith in someone who frequently cancels plans or, worse yet, lies.

Make plans and carry them out. If you're unsure whether you'll be able to attend the dinner, don't say yes. Instead, take responsibility. When you and your partner are making plans, keep a calendar and refer to it often. Don't promise to call only to forget to. Set a phone reminder in its place. Being dependable shows that you value the time and emotions of your spouse. After all, having your plans repeatedly altered might be difficult.

There will inevitably be occasions when you have no choice but to cancel—a family emergency, a sickness, or the need to study for a significant test. Regarding these conditions, you shouldn't feel guilty (or be persuaded to feel guilty!). However, it can be quite helpful if you demonstrate that you are conscious of the impact those behaviors (whether they are under your control or not) have on your spouse. When you're free, make sure to check in with them and apologize. You should also offer to reschedule.

4. Encourage solitude.
When you first start dating, you could be so eager to spend every moment with your spouse. That is entirely typical. The other significant relationships in your life, such as those with your family and friends, might, however, be simple to overlook. No one person can meet all of your social and emotional needs, no matter how wonderful they are. And every now and again, everyone needs a break from their significant other. You can both continue to develop as humans by spending time alone or with others. Your partnership may remain fascinating by incorporating new concepts and activities from both of you. You each get an opportunity to discuss how you get along with your friends and family. Who wouldn't want to extol their new love a little?

5. Respect one another's differences.
Never belittle your partner's opinions or pursuits. Even if you don't agree with someone, you can respect their viewpoint.

Relationships are fantastic because of their contrasts, in part! Even if you don't finally change your mind, your partner can help you see the world from a different angle. Even if you would never step foot in a baseball stadium or art gallery otherwise, you may show your spouse that you value them by attending their baseball game or art exhibit.

Even if your partner has different boundaries than you, respect them. Don't pressurize your partner if they don't want to have sex, kiss in public, or lie to their parents. This is possibly harsh and coercive.

6. Discover who you are.

You're not just getting to know someone while you're in a relationship. You're learning more about who you are. Finding out what you want and need from the people in your life can be aided by being in a committed relationship. What are you prepared to give up? Which traits of yours go well with them? Which of your key principles are inviolable? Perhaps you don't mind if your spouse doesn't enjoy R&B music as much as you do, but you can't tolerate it when they treat your cat cruelly. Learn more about who you are as a partner and as a person. Knowing oneself improves communication, something your partner will undoubtedly value.

Knowing your personal limits makes it far simpler to recognize when those limits have been violated and when a relationship should be terminated.

It may sound difficult to show respect, but it's really not.
It all boils down to paying attention to and being kind to your mate. You can be in an abusive relationship if your spouse constantly asks you where you are, accuses you of lying or cheating, berates you, calls you names, or engages in any kind of physical violence. Abusive relationships are

built on control and power rather than on respect.

Chapter 5: MAINTAINING THEIR LOVE

Although it's always exciting and wonderful to start a relationship, maintaining one over the long term requires effort. Once you've established your connection, it's important to keep the lines of communication open and to continue to value the time spent with your partner. Making a relationship last can be challenging, but the rewards of having a committed, long-term relationship far surpass any challenges you may encounter. Just heed the advice in this article if you want to know how to keep your relationship strong.

Be grateful to your partner. Never assume anything about the other person. If you fall in love, you'll need to put in the effort to keep that person interested in you. Never, ever taking someone for granted is the best method to keep them in love with you. Make

sure to let the person know every day how much you value them.
Say "thank you" when your partner does something kind for you, for instance. The "thank you" should be honest and precise. For instance, "Thank you for preparing the coffee this morning and putting the dishes away! My morning was so much simpler as a result! I'm incredibly grateful for it.

Spend time together as a couple. You shouldn't give up just because you two are in love and your relationship appears to be strong and at its best. Continue having dates, purchasing flowers for one another, and similar activities. This will demonstrate to your partner that you still value and are committed to the union.
The most important thing is to tell your partner that you love them every day.

Keep the action frantic. Don't just carry on with what you normally do. Routines can be enjoyable, soothing, and even comforting, but it's crucial to occasionally shake them up and do something fun and novel with your loved ones. This demonstrates to your partner that there are still things to look forward to in the relationship and that being with you won't make their lives stagnant. Additionally, it can aid in relieving some of the exhilaration of first love.

Try something risky, like rock climbing or skydiving. enroll in dance courses or take up painting lessons together.

Learn something new together, such as how to construct furniture, and use it to fill your home with items you both made.

Consider starting a board game night so you may enjoy yourselves with each other and indulge your competitive tendencies.

Chapter 6: BEGINNING A ROMANCE

What Is Love?

Romance is a state of being or a behavior used to express a shared romantic or love-like desire. Numerous cultures have associated romance with the idea of "real love" between lovers throughout history, as evidenced through literature, music, art, and other forms of expression. Valentine's Day is a day set aside to honor this idea.

As the lovers get to know one another, romance may start as a mutual attraction and grow into something more intense and consummate. Both parties must frequently express their love for one another through romantic acts for this kind of relationship to be healthy.

The Art of Romance

There are various methods to show someone you care, whether you wish to find romantic love or develop an already close relationship. Some examples include:

Find the appropriate person for you. Your likelihood of being able to fall in love, be loved, and stay in love will increase if you find the perfect person. The person you pick must be compatible with you, prepared for a committed relationship, and able to handle the emotional strain of being in a committed relationship. If the applicant does not match these criteria, your time will be wasted, and you run the risk of getting wounded.
Consider your compatibility: Do you share the same interests? Do you share the same life objectives? In terms of how they handle conflict and what they value in life, people who make good couples often have similar traits.

Make a date. Don't mince words when asking someone out; be direct and detailed. Be honest about your reasons for wanting the person to attend and propose a specific

activity that will be fun for both of you. This kind of assertive behavior demonstrates your confidence, which is a positive attribute.
Say something like, "Hey, I really want to go to the zoo this weekend and I would love it if you would be my date." to your particular someone.

Be a fantastic date. You should be a fun person to be around right from the first date. You should make plans to spend time together in a way that showcases how lovely you are even before your date.
Pick date activities that you and your partner will enjoy. Choose an activity that will give you and your date something to chat about, like as a movie, if you don't know each other very well. If you do get along well, pick an activity that is unusual for both of you. They might view you differently as a result of this.

Try going on an exciting date, such as an action movie or amusement park. It has been demonstrated that engaging in these activities makes two people more attracted to one another.

Bottom line

You can't force something as life-changing as love and it doesn't happen overnight. The best kind of love is unexpected, if it is meant to be it will happen naturally. If you try to force someone to love you, it will most likely have the opposite effect.

Don't be clingy or pushy with someone who's rejected your feelings. Anyone that you have to try too hard to convince to like you is not worth all the trouble and will probably never like you. Pursuing a relationship too hard will only make you creepy and push people further away.

This guide is not guaranteed to make someone fall in love with you. If you do all of the things discussed above and they still don’t love you, then they are probably incapable of loving you (or already in love with someone else) and the two of you were a poor match. Some people are simply incompatible, even if one person feels very strongly about the other. It may be hard to hear, but you are better off ending a relationship if the other person simply cannot return your feelings.

Don’t buy into the idea that you can use a certain pheromone, chemical spray, or food to make someone fall in love with you. While there is scientific evidence that such things affect the parts of our brain which deal with those emotions, these chemicals will not force someone to fall in love with you. There is no foolproof “love potion” as it were.

www.ingramcontent.com/pod-product-compliance
Lightning Source LLC
LaVergne TN
LVHW020525160826
845677LV00015B/3906

* 9 7 9 8 3 6 6 4 1 6 3 1 3 *